50 Taiwanese Soul Food Recipes

By: Kelly Johnson

Table of Contents

- Lu Rou Fan (Braised Pork Rice)
- Taiwanese Beef Noodle Soup
- Gua Bao (Pork Belly Buns)
- Taiwanese Popcorn Chicken
- Taiwanese Oysters Omelette
- Stinky Tofu
- Three-Cup Chicken
- Taiwanese Egg Pancake
- Pork Chop with Rice
- Taiwanese Meatball Soup
- Fried Sweet Potato Balls
- Hot and Sour Soup
- Taiwanese Style Dumplings
- Taiwanese Sausage with Garlic
- Peanut Soup with Mochi
- Pineapple Cake
- Spicy Duck Blood Soup

- Taiwanese Soy Milk Breakfast Set
- Sweet and Sour Chicken
- Taiwanese Sticky Rice with Dried Shrimp
- Braised Pork with Tofu
- Scallion Oil Noodles
- Taiwanese Fish Ball Soup
- Taiwanese-style Bubble Tea
- Dan Zai Noodles
- Salt and Pepper Shrimp
- Taiwanese Watercress Soup
- Sweet Potato Soup
- Taiwanese Stewed Pork Hock
- Taiwanese Fried Rice
- Red Bean Soup with Tapioca
- Pickled Mustard Greens with Pork
- Taiwanese Hot Pot
- Taiwan Beef Stir Fry
- Taiwanese Tofu Salad
- Taiwanese Rice Dumplings (Zongzi)

- Fried Taiwanese Pancakes
- Baked Tofu with Sweet Soy
- Taiwanese Braised Pork Over Rice
- Tainan-style Meat Soup
- Pineapple Shrimp Balls
- Taiwanese Hot Dog with Garlic
- Pork and Chinese Cabbage Stew
- Sweet Soy Braised Chicken
- Roasted Eggplant with Soy Sauce
- Taiwanese Fried Stinky Tofu
- Glutinous Rice Balls with Black Sesame
- Fried Taro Balls
- Ginger Pork Soup
- Red Yeast Rice Pork Belly

Lu Rou Fan (Braised Pork Rice)

Ingredients:

- 1 lb ground pork
- 2 tbsp soy sauce
- 1 tbsp dark soy sauce
- 1 tbsp rice wine
- 1 tbsp sugar
- 1/2 cup water
- 2 cloves garlic, minced
- 1/2 onion, chopped
- 2 boiled eggs (optional)
- Steamed rice

Instructions:

1. In a pan, brown the ground pork.
2. Add garlic, onion, soy sauce, dark soy sauce, rice wine, sugar, and water. Stir and bring to a simmer.
3. Cover and braise for 1–1.5 hours, stirring occasionally.
4. Serve the braised pork over steamed rice and top with boiled eggs.

Taiwanese Beef Noodle Soup

Ingredients:

- 1 lb beef shank or short ribs
- 4 cups beef broth
- 2 tbsp soy sauce
- 1 tbsp rice wine
- 2 cloves garlic, minced
- 1-inch ginger, sliced
- 1 tbsp star anise
- 1 tbsp sugar
- 4-5 slices bok choy or spinach
- 4 oz egg noodles

Instructions:

1. In a pot, brown beef pieces, then add beef broth, soy sauce, rice wine, garlic, ginger, star anise, and sugar.
2. Bring to a boil, then reduce to a simmer and cook for 2 hours until the beef is tender.
3. Cook egg noodles according to package instructions.
4. Serve the beef soup over noodles and top with bok choy.

Gua Bao (Pork Belly Buns)

Ingredients:

- 1 lb pork belly
- 2 tbsp soy sauce
- 1 tbsp rice wine
- 1 tbsp sugar
- 2 cloves garlic, minced
- 1 tbsp five-spice powder
- Steamed bao buns
- Fresh cilantro, pickled mustard greens, and crushed peanuts for garnish

Instructions:

1. Brown pork belly in a pan, then add soy sauce, rice wine, sugar, garlic, and five-spice powder. Simmer for 1–1.5 hours until the pork is tender.
2. Slice the cooked pork belly and place it in steamed bao buns.
3. Garnish with cilantro, pickled mustard greens, and crushed peanuts before serving.

Taiwanese Popcorn Chicken

Ingredients:

- 1 lb chicken thighs, cut into bite-sized pieces
- 2 tbsp soy sauce
- 1 tbsp rice wine
- 1 tbsp sugar
- 1 tsp five-spice powder
- 1 tbsp cornstarch
- 1 egg, beaten
- Oil for frying
- Thai basil leaves (optional)

Instructions:

1. Marinate the chicken with soy sauce, rice wine, sugar, and five-spice powder for 30 minutes.
2. Dredge the marinated chicken pieces in cornstarch, then dip in beaten egg.
3. Heat oil in a pan and fry the chicken until golden brown and crispy.
4. Optional: Fry some Thai basil leaves in the oil for added flavor and garnish. Serve the chicken with basil.

Taiwanese Oysters Omelette

Ingredients:

- 1/2 lb fresh oysters
- 2 eggs, beaten
- 1/2 cup tapioca starch (or cornstarch)
- 1 cup water
- 1 tbsp soy sauce
- 1 tbsp rice vinegar
- 1 tsp sugar
- 1/4 cup cilantro, chopped
- Oil for frying

Instructions:

1. Mix tapioca starch and water to create a slurry.
2. Heat oil in a pan, add oysters, and cook for 2 minutes.
3. Pour in the starch slurry and cook until it thickens into a jelly-like consistency.
4. Add beaten eggs and cook until set, then flip to cook the other side.
5. Mix soy sauce, rice vinegar, and sugar to make a sauce.
6. Serve the omelette topped with cilantro and the sauce.

Stinky Tofu

Ingredients:

- 1 block of fermented tofu (stinky tofu)
- Oil for deep frying
- 1 tbsp soy sauce
- 1 tbsp rice vinegar
- 1 tsp sugar
- Chili sauce or pickled cabbage (optional)

Instructions:

1. Heat oil in a deep fryer or large pan.
2. Deep fry the tofu until golden brown and crispy.
3. Mix soy sauce, rice vinegar, and sugar to create a dipping sauce.
4. Serve the stinky tofu with chili sauce or pickled cabbage.

Three-Cup Chicken

Ingredients:

- 1 lb chicken thighs, cut into pieces
- 2 tbsp soy sauce
- 2 tbsp rice wine
- 2 tbsp sesame oil
- 3 cloves garlic, minced
- 1-inch ginger, sliced
- 1/4 cup fresh basil leaves

Instructions:

1. Heat sesame oil in a pan, then sauté garlic and ginger until fragrant.
2. Add chicken and cook until browned.
3. Stir in soy sauce, rice wine, and sugar, then simmer for 15–20 minutes.
4. Add fresh basil leaves just before serving, and serve over rice.

Taiwanese Egg Pancake

Ingredients:

- 1/2 cup flour
- 1/4 cup water
- 1 egg
- 2 tbsp soy sauce
- 1 tsp sesame oil
- 1/4 cup green onions, chopped
- Oil for frying

Instructions:

1. Mix flour, water, egg, soy sauce, and sesame oil to form a thin batter.
2. Heat a pan and add a little oil. Pour a thin layer of batter into the pan and cook until golden.
3. Sprinkle with green onions, fold, and serve hot.

Pork Chop with Rice

Ingredients:

- 2 pork chops
- 2 tbsp soy sauce
- 1 tbsp rice wine
- 1 tbsp sugar
- 2 cloves garlic, minced
- Steamed rice

Instructions:

1. Marinate the pork chops with soy sauce, rice wine, garlic, and sugar for 30 minutes.
2. Grill or pan-fry the pork chops until cooked through and golden brown.
3. Serve with steamed rice on the side.

Taiwanese Meatball Soup

Ingredients:

- 1 lb ground pork
- 1/4 cup bamboo shoots, chopped
- 1/4 cup water chestnuts, chopped
- 2 tbsp soy sauce
- 1 tbsp rice wine
- 1 tbsp cornstarch
- 4 cups chicken broth
- 2-3 slices ginger
- 1/4 tsp white pepper
- 2 green onions, chopped

Instructions:

1. Mix the ground pork, bamboo shoots, water chestnuts, soy sauce, rice wine, cornstarch, and white pepper to form meatballs.
2. In a pot, bring the chicken broth to a simmer with ginger slices.
3. Drop the meatballs into the broth and cook until they float, about 10 minutes.
4. Garnish with green onions before serving.

Fried Sweet Potato Balls

Ingredients:

- 2 cups sweet potato, mashed
- 1/2 cup tapioca starch
- 1/4 cup sugar
- 1/4 tsp salt
- Oil for frying

Instructions:

1. Mix mashed sweet potato, tapioca starch, sugar, and salt to form a dough.
2. Roll the dough into small balls.
3. Heat oil in a pan and deep fry the sweet potato balls until golden brown and crispy.
4. Drain excess oil and serve.

Hot and Sour Soup

Ingredients:

- 4 cups chicken broth
- 1/2 cup wood ear mushrooms, sliced
- 1/2 cup shiitake mushrooms, sliced
- 1/4 cup tofu, cubed
- 1/4 cup bamboo shoots, sliced
- 2 tbsp soy sauce
- 1 tbsp rice vinegar
- 1 tsp sugar
- 1 tbsp cornstarch (mixed with 1 tbsp water)
- 1/4 tsp white pepper
- 1 egg, beaten
- Green onions for garnish

Instructions:

1. Bring the chicken broth to a simmer in a pot.
2. Add mushrooms, tofu, bamboo shoots, soy sauce, rice vinegar, sugar, and white pepper.
3. Simmer for 5 minutes, then stir in the cornstarch mixture to thicken the soup.
4. Slowly pour in the beaten egg while stirring to create egg ribbons.

5. Garnish with green onions and serve hot.

Taiwanese Style Dumplings

Ingredients:

- 1 lb ground pork
- 1/4 cup napa cabbage, chopped
- 1/4 cup shiitake mushrooms, finely chopped
- 1 tbsp soy sauce
- 1 tbsp rice wine
- 1 tsp ginger, minced
- 1 tsp sesame oil
- 1 package dumpling wrappers

Instructions:

1. Combine ground pork, cabbage, mushrooms, soy sauce, rice wine, ginger, and sesame oil in a bowl.
2. Place a small amount of filling in the center of each dumpling wrapper and fold to seal.
3. Steam or pan-fry the dumplings until golden brown and cooked through.
4. Serve with soy sauce or chili oil.

Taiwanese Sausage with Garlic

Ingredients:

- 4 Taiwanese sausages
- 3 cloves garlic, minced
- 1 tbsp soy sauce
- 1 tbsp rice wine
- 1 tsp sugar
- 2-3 sprigs cilantro, chopped

Instructions:

1. Grill or pan-fry the Taiwanese sausages until cooked through.
2. In a separate pan, sauté garlic in oil until fragrant.
3. Add soy sauce, rice wine, and sugar to the garlic and simmer for a few minutes.
4. Serve sausages with garlic sauce and garnish with chopped cilantro.

Peanut Soup with Mochi

Ingredients:

- 1 cup roasted peanuts, ground
- 4 cups water
- 1/4 cup sugar
- 1/4 tsp salt
- 1/2 cup glutinous rice flour
- Water for mochi dough

Instructions:

1. In a pot, combine ground peanuts, water, sugar, and salt. Bring to a boil and simmer for 15 minutes.
2. In a bowl, mix glutinous rice flour with enough water to form a dough.
3. Roll dough into small balls and drop them into the boiling peanut soup. Cook until the mochi balls float.
4. Serve the peanut soup with mochi balls.

Pineapple Cake

Ingredients:

- 2 cups all-purpose flour
- 1/2 cup unsalted butter
- 1/4 cup powdered sugar
- 1 egg
- 1/2 tsp vanilla extract
- 1/4 tsp salt
- 1 cup pineapple jam (store-bought or homemade)

Instructions:

1. Cream butter and powdered sugar in a bowl. Add the egg, vanilla, salt, and flour, and mix until a dough forms.

2. Roll the dough into small portions and shape them into small squares.

3. Place a teaspoon of pineapple jam in the center of each square and fold the dough to seal.

4. Bake at 350°F (175°C) for 15–20 minutes or until golden brown.

Spicy Duck Blood Soup

Ingredients:

- 2 cups duck blood (or tofu if unavailable)
- 4 cups chicken or duck broth
- 1 tbsp soy sauce
- 1 tbsp rice vinegar
- 1 tsp chili paste
- 1/4 tsp white pepper
- 1/2 cup spinach or bok choy
- 2 cloves garlic, minced

Instructions:

1. Bring the broth to a boil, then add soy sauce, rice vinegar, chili paste, and white pepper.
2. Cut duck blood into small cubes and add them to the soup.
3. Simmer for 10–15 minutes.
4. Add garlic and spinach or bok choy, cooking until wilted.
5. Serve hot with additional chili paste if desired.

Taiwanese Soy Milk Breakfast Set

Ingredients:

- 2 cups soy milk
- 2 boiled eggs
- 1-2 crispy fried dough sticks (Youtiao)
- Pickled vegetables (optional)
- Soy sauce and sugar for dipping

Instructions:

1. Heat the soy milk in a pot and bring it to a simmer.
2. Serve the soy milk with boiled eggs and crispy fried dough sticks on the side.
3. Garnish with pickled vegetables and dip the dough sticks in a mixture of soy sauce and sugar.

Sweet and Sour Chicken

Ingredients:

- 1 lb chicken breast, cut into cubes
- 1/4 cup cornstarch
- 1/4 cup flour
- Oil for frying
- 1/4 cup rice vinegar
- 1/4 cup ketchup
- 1/4 cup sugar
- 1/4 cup soy sauce
- 1/4 cup bell peppers, chopped
- 1/4 cup pineapple chunks

Instructions:

1. Toss chicken cubes in cornstarch and flour.
2. Heat oil in a pan and fry the chicken until golden brown.
3. In a separate pan, mix rice vinegar, ketchup, sugar, and soy sauce to create the sweet and sour sauce.
4. Add bell peppers and pineapple to the sauce, simmering until tender.
5. Combine the fried chicken with the sauce and serve hot.

Taiwanese Sticky Rice with Dried Shrimp

Ingredients:

- 2 cups sticky rice (glutinous rice), soaked for 2 hours
- 1/4 cup dried shrimp, soaked in warm water for 30 minutes
- 1/4 cup shiitake mushrooms, sliced
- 1/4 cup Chinese sausage, sliced
- 2 tbsp soy sauce
- 1 tbsp oyster sauce
- 1 tbsp sesame oil
- 1/4 tsp white pepper
- 1/2 cup chicken stock
- 2-3 leaves of dried lotus leaf (optional)

Instructions:

1. Drain the soaked sticky rice and set it aside.
2. In a pan, heat sesame oil and sauté the dried shrimp, mushrooms, and Chinese sausage until fragrant.
3. Add the sticky rice to the pan and stir to coat with the flavors.
4. Stir in the soy sauce, oyster sauce, white pepper, and chicken stock.
5. Wrap the rice mixture in lotus leaves (if using), or place it directly in a rice cooker to steam for 30-40 minutes until fully cooked.

6. Serve hot.

Braised Pork with Tofu

Ingredients:

- 1 lb pork belly, cut into chunks
- 1 block firm tofu, cut into cubes
- 3 tbsp soy sauce
- 2 tbsp rice wine
- 2 tbsp sugar
- 2 slices ginger
- 3-4 dried Chinese mushrooms (optional)
- 2 cups water
- 1 tbsp cornstarch (optional, for thickening)

Instructions:

1. In a pot, heat some oil and brown the pork belly chunks.
2. Add ginger and dried mushrooms, sautéing for 2-3 minutes.
3. Stir in soy sauce, rice wine, sugar, and water. Bring to a simmer.
4. Add tofu cubes and continue to braise for 40-50 minutes, until pork is tender and the sauce has reduced.
5. If desired, thicken the sauce by mixing cornstarch with water and adding it to the pot.
6. Serve hot with steamed rice.

Scallion Oil Noodles

Ingredients:

- 1 lb fresh egg noodles (or other noodles)
- 3 tbsp sesame oil
- 1/4 cup vegetable oil
- 5-6 scallions, finely chopped
- 2 tbsp soy sauce
- 1 tbsp sugar
- 1 tbsp rice vinegar

Instructions:

1. Cook the noodles according to the package instructions. Drain and set aside.
2. In a pan, heat vegetable oil and sesame oil. Add the chopped scallions and cook over medium heat until fragrant and slightly crispy.
3. Stir in soy sauce, sugar, and rice vinegar, and let the mixture simmer for 1-2 minutes.
4. Toss the cooked noodles in the scallion oil sauce, ensuring they are well-coated.
5. Serve immediately.

Taiwanese Fish Ball Soup

Ingredients:

- 10-12 Taiwanese fish balls (store-bought or homemade)
- 4 cups chicken or fish broth
- 1 tbsp soy sauce
- 1 tbsp rice wine
- 2-3 slices ginger
- 1/4 cup napa cabbage, shredded
- 2 green onions, chopped

Instructions:

1. Bring the broth to a boil in a pot, then add the ginger, soy sauce, and rice wine.
2. Drop the fish balls into the broth and cook for 5-7 minutes until they float.
3. Add the shredded napa cabbage and cook until tender, about 2 minutes.
4. Garnish with chopped green onions and serve hot.

Taiwanese-style Bubble Tea

Ingredients:

- 2 cups brewed black tea, chilled
- 1/2 cup tapioca pearls
- 1/2 cup milk (or non-dairy milk)
- 2 tbsp sugar or honey (adjust to taste)

Instructions:

1. Cook the tapioca pearls according to package instructions.
2. In a glass, combine the chilled tea, milk, and sugar. Stir until the sugar dissolves.
3. Add the cooked tapioca pearls to the bottom of the glass.
4. Pour the tea mixture over the pearls and stir.
5. Serve with a wide straw and enjoy!

Dan Zai Noodles

Ingredients:

- 1/2 lb fresh egg noodles
- 1/4 lb ground pork
- 2 tbsp soy sauce
- 1 tbsp rice wine
- 1 tbsp sugar
- 1/4 cup chicken broth
- 1/2 tsp sesame oil
- 1/4 tsp white pepper
- 2-3 green onions, chopped
- Pickled mustard greens (optional)

Instructions:

1. Cook the noodles according to package instructions. Drain and set aside.
2. In a pan, sauté the ground pork until browned.
3. Add soy sauce, rice wine, sugar, chicken broth, sesame oil, and white pepper. Let it simmer for 5-7 minutes.
4. Place the cooked noodles in bowls, pour the pork mixture over the top, and garnish with green onions and pickled mustard greens.
5. Serve immediately.

Salt and Pepper Shrimp

Ingredients:

- 1 lb shrimp, peeled and deveined
- 1/4 cup cornstarch
- 1/4 cup flour
- 1 tsp white pepper
- 1 tsp salt
- Oil for frying
- 2 cloves garlic, minced
- 1-2 dried chili peppers (optional)
- 2-3 sprigs cilantro, chopped

Instructions:

1. Mix cornstarch, flour, white pepper, and salt in a bowl.
2. Toss the shrimp in the flour mixture, coating evenly.
3. Heat oil in a pan and fry the shrimp until golden and crispy.
4. In another pan, sauté garlic and dried chili peppers (if using) until fragrant.
5. Toss the fried shrimp in the garlic and chili mixture and garnish with chopped cilantro.
6. Serve hot.

Taiwanese Watercress Soup

Ingredients:

- 4 cups chicken or pork broth
- 2 cups watercress, washed and chopped
- 1/2 lb pork ribs or chicken (optional)
- 2-3 slices ginger
- 1 tbsp soy sauce
- 1 tsp rice wine
- 1/4 tsp white pepper

Instructions:

1. Bring the broth to a boil and add pork ribs or chicken (if using).
2. Add ginger, soy sauce, rice wine, and white pepper, and simmer for 30-40 minutes.
3. Add the chopped watercress and cook for another 5-10 minutes.
4. Serve hot.

Sweet Potato Soup

Ingredients:

- 2 medium sweet potatoes, peeled and cubed
- 4 cups water or chicken broth
- 1/4 cup sugar
- 1/4 tsp salt
- 2-3 slices ginger (optional)
- 1 tbsp cornstarch (optional, for thickening)

Instructions:

1. In a pot, combine the sweet potatoes and water (or chicken broth).
2. Bring to a boil and simmer for 20-30 minutes, or until the sweet potatoes are tender.
3. Add sugar, salt, and ginger slices (if using), and continue to simmer for another 5 minutes.
4. For a thicker soup, mix cornstarch with water and add to the pot. Stir until thickened.
5. Serve hot.

Taiwanese Stewed Pork Hock

Ingredients:

- 2 pork hocks
- 2 tbsp soy sauce
- 1 tbsp rice wine
- 2 tbsp sugar
- 3-4 slices ginger
- 2-3 star anise
- 4-5 dried Chinese mushrooms (optional)
- 4 cups water

Instructions:

1. In a large pot, brown the pork hocks on all sides.
2. Add soy sauce, rice wine, sugar, ginger, star anise, dried mushrooms (if using), and water.
3. Bring to a boil, then reduce heat and simmer for 1.5-2 hours, until the meat is tender and the flavors are absorbed.
4. Serve hot with steamed rice.

Taiwanese Fried Rice

Ingredients:

- 2 cups cooked jasmine rice (preferably cold)
- 1/4 cup diced ham or Chinese sausage
- 2 eggs, beaten
- 1/4 cup green peas
- 2 green onions, chopped
- 1/4 cup soy sauce
- 1 tbsp oyster sauce
- 1 tbsp sesame oil
- 1/4 tsp white pepper
- 2 cloves garlic, minced
- 1 tbsp vegetable oil

Instructions:

1. Heat vegetable oil in a wok or large pan over medium heat.
2. Add garlic and diced ham or sausage, stir-frying for 1-2 minutes until fragrant.
3. Push the meat to one side of the pan and scramble the eggs on the other side.
4. Add the cold rice to the pan and break up any clumps. Stir-fry for 3-4 minutes.
5. Stir in the soy sauce, oyster sauce, sesame oil, white pepper, and green peas. Cook for another 2-3 minutes.

6. Add green onions, and stir well. Serve hot.

Red Bean Soup with Tapioca

Ingredients:

- 1 cup red beans (azuki beans)
- 1/4 cup small tapioca pearls
- 1/2 cup rock sugar (adjust to taste)
- 4 cups water
- 1-2 slices of orange peel (optional)

Instructions:

1. Rinse the red beans and soak them in water for 4 hours or overnight.
2. In a large pot, bring the water to a boil. Add the soaked beans and simmer for 30 minutes.
3. Stir in the tapioca pearls and orange peel (if using), and simmer for another 30 minutes, or until the beans are soft and the tapioca pearls become translucent.
4. Sweeten with rock sugar to taste. Stir until dissolved.
5. Serve hot or chilled, as a refreshing dessert.

Pickled Mustard Greens with Pork

Ingredients:

- 1/2 lb pork belly, thinly sliced
- 1/2 cup pickled mustard greens, rinsed and chopped
- 2 cloves garlic, minced
- 1 tbsp soy sauce
- 1 tbsp rice wine
- 1 tbsp sugar
- 1 tbsp vegetable oil
- 1/2 tsp white pepper
- 2-3 sprigs cilantro for garnish

Instructions:

1. Heat vegetable oil in a pan over medium heat. Add minced garlic and sauté until fragrant.
2. Add the pork belly slices and cook until browned and crispy.
3. Stir in soy sauce, rice wine, sugar, and white pepper. Cook for 5-7 minutes, allowing the pork to absorb the flavors.
4. Add the pickled mustard greens, stir, and cook for another 2-3 minutes.
5. Garnish with fresh cilantro before serving.

Taiwanese Hot Pot

Ingredients:

- 1 lb thinly sliced beef, lamb, or chicken
- 1/2 lb tofu, cut into cubes
- 1/2 lb mushrooms (shiitake, enoki, or any variety)
- 2 cups napa cabbage, chopped
- 1/4 cup soy sauce
- 2 tbsp rice wine
- 2 tbsp sesame oil
- 1 tbsp chili paste (optional)
- 6 cups chicken or vegetable broth
- 2 green onions, chopped
- 2-3 slices ginger

Instructions:

1. In a large pot, bring the broth to a simmer. Add soy sauce, rice wine, sesame oil, and ginger slices.
2. Add the tofu, mushrooms, napa cabbage, and any other desired vegetables. Simmer for 10-15 minutes.
3. Arrange the thinly sliced meat on a platter. Serve the hot pot with dipping sauces such as chili paste, soy sauce, and sesame oil.
4. To eat, dip the raw meat into the hot broth and cook for 1-2 minutes until tender.

5. Garnish with green onions before serving.

Taiwan Beef Stir Fry

Ingredients:

- 1 lb beef (sirloin or flank steak), thinly sliced against the grain
- 2 tbsp soy sauce
- 1 tbsp rice wine
- 1 tbsp oyster sauce
- 1 tbsp sugar
- 2 cloves garlic, minced
- 1 onion, sliced
- 1 bell pepper, sliced
- 1 tbsp cornstarch (for marinating)
- 1/4 tsp white pepper
- 2 tbsp vegetable oil
- 1-2 green onions, chopped

Instructions:

1. In a bowl, mix the sliced beef with soy sauce, rice wine, oyster sauce, sugar, cornstarch, and white pepper. Let it marinate for 20-30 minutes.
2. Heat vegetable oil in a wok or pan over medium-high heat.
3. Add garlic and onion, stir-fry for 2-3 minutes until fragrant.
4. Add the marinated beef and stir-fry until it is cooked through (about 3-4 minutes).

5. Toss in bell peppers and continue stir-frying for another 2 minutes.

6. Garnish with chopped green onions and serve immediately with rice.

Taiwanese Tofu Salad

Ingredients:

- 1 block firm tofu, cut into cubes
- 1 cucumber, thinly sliced
- 1/2 cup shredded carrots
- 1 tbsp soy sauce
- 1 tbsp rice vinegar
- 1 tbsp sesame oil
- 1 tsp sugar
- 1/2 tsp chili oil (optional)
- 1 tbsp sesame seeds
- Fresh cilantro for garnish

Instructions:

1. Arrange the tofu, cucumber, and shredded carrots in a bowl.
2. In a small bowl, mix soy sauce, rice vinegar, sesame oil, sugar, and chili oil (if using).
3. Pour the dressing over the tofu and vegetables, gently tossing to coat.
4. Sprinkle sesame seeds and garnish with fresh cilantro before serving.

Taiwanese Rice Dumplings (Zongzi)

Ingredients:

- 2 cups glutinous rice, soaked for 2-3 hours
- 6-8 dried bamboo leaves, soaked in warm water
- 1/2 lb pork belly, cubed
- 1/4 cup salted egg yolks, sliced
- 1/4 cup dried shrimp, soaked
- 1 tbsp soy sauce
- 1 tbsp rice wine
- 1 tbsp sugar
- 1/4 tsp five-spice powder
- 1/4 cup chestnuts (optional)

Instructions:

1. Season the pork belly with soy sauce, rice wine, sugar, and five-spice powder. Let it marinate for 30 minutes.
2. Lay two bamboo leaves on top of each other to form a cross and spoon some soaked rice onto the leaves.
3. Add a few pieces of marinated pork, salted egg yolk, dried shrimp, and chestnuts (if using) on top.
4. Fold the leaves to form a triangular or rectangular shape and tie securely with string.

5. Steam the dumplings for 2-3 hours until the rice is fully cooked.

6. Serve hot.

Fried Taiwanese Pancakes

Ingredients:

- 1 1/2 cups all-purpose flour
- 1/2 tsp salt
- 1/2 tsp sugar
- 3/4 cup warm water
- 1 tbsp sesame oil
- 1/4 cup green onions, chopped
- Vegetable oil for frying

Instructions:

1. Mix flour, salt, and sugar in a bowl. Gradually add warm water to form a dough.
2. Knead the dough for 5-7 minutes, then cover and let it rest for 30 minutes.
3. Roll the dough into a flat circle. Brush with sesame oil and sprinkle with green onions.
4. Roll the dough up and shape it into a coil. Roll it out again into a flat circle.
5. Heat oil in a pan and fry the pancakes on both sides until golden and crispy.
6. Serve warm.

Baked Tofu with Sweet Soy

Ingredients:

- 1 block firm tofu, cut into slices
- 2 tbsp soy sauce
- 1 tbsp honey or sugar
- 1 tbsp sesame oil
- 1 tbsp rice vinegar
- 1 tsp cornstarch
- 1 tsp sesame seeds
- Fresh cilantro for garnish

Instructions:

1. Preheat the oven to 375°F (190°C). Line a baking sheet with parchment paper.
2. Arrange tofu slices on the baking sheet.
3. In a bowl, whisk together soy sauce, honey, sesame oil, rice vinegar, and cornstarch to make the sauce.
4. Brush the sauce over the tofu slices and bake for 25-30 minutes until golden and crispy.
5. Garnish with sesame seeds and fresh cilantro before serving.

Taiwanese Braised Pork Over Rice

Ingredients:

- 1 lb pork belly, cubed
- 2 tbsp soy sauce
- 2 tbsp rice wine
- 1 tbsp sugar
- 3-4 cloves garlic, minced
- 1/2 tsp five-spice powder
- 2-3 slices ginger
- 2-3 boiled eggs (optional)
- Steamed rice for serving

Instructions:

1. Heat oil in a pot and brown the pork belly cubes.
2. Add garlic, ginger, soy sauce, rice wine, sugar, and five-spice powder. Stir well.
3. Add enough water to cover the pork and simmer for 1-1.5 hours until tender.
4. Add boiled eggs to the pot for the last 30 minutes if using.
5. Serve the braised pork over steamed rice, garnished with extra sauce.

Tainan-style Meat Soup

Ingredients:

- 1 lb ground pork or beef
- 1/2 lb tofu, cut into cubes
- 1/4 cup sliced shiitake mushrooms
- 4 cups chicken broth
- 2 tbsp soy sauce
- 1 tbsp rice wine
- 1 tbsp sugar
- 1 tbsp cornstarch (for thickening)
- 1 tbsp sesame oil
- 1/4 tsp white pepper
- 2 green onions, chopped (for garnish)

Instructions:

1. Heat sesame oil in a pot over medium heat. Add ground meat and cook until browned, breaking it up as it cooks.
2. Add the shiitake mushrooms and tofu cubes, cooking for another 2-3 minutes.
3. Pour in the chicken broth, soy sauce, rice wine, and sugar. Bring to a boil, then reduce heat to a simmer.
4. In a small bowl, mix cornstarch with a little water to form a slurry, then stir into the soup to thicken it slightly.

5. Let it simmer for 10-15 minutes, then season with white pepper to taste.

6. Garnish with chopped green onions and serve hot.

Pineapple Shrimp Balls

Ingredients:

- 1 lb shrimp, peeled and deveined
- 1/2 cup breadcrumbs
- 1/4 cup fresh pineapple, finely chopped
- 1 egg
- 2 tbsp cornstarch
- 1 tbsp soy sauce
- 1 tbsp sesame oil
- 1/4 tsp white pepper
- 1/4 tsp salt
- Vegetable oil for frying

Instructions:

1. In a food processor, pulse the shrimp until finely chopped but not pureed. Transfer to a bowl.
2. Add breadcrumbs, pineapple, egg, cornstarch, soy sauce, sesame oil, white pepper, and salt. Mix until well combined.
3. Form the mixture into small balls, about the size of a golf ball.
4. Heat vegetable oil in a frying pan over medium heat. Fry the shrimp balls in batches for 3-4 minutes until golden brown and cooked through.
5. Remove from the oil and drain on paper towels. Serve hot.

Taiwanese Hot Dog with Garlic

Ingredients:

- 4 Taiwanese-style hot dog sausages
- 4 hot dog buns
- 2 tbsp garlic, minced
- 2 tbsp soy sauce
- 1 tbsp sugar
- 1 tbsp rice vinegar
- 1 tbsp sesame oil
- 1/4 tsp chili flakes (optional)
- 1/4 cup chopped cilantro
- Pickled mustard greens (optional, for topping)

Instructions:

1. In a small pan, heat sesame oil over medium heat and sauté the minced garlic until fragrant, about 1-2 minutes.
2. Add soy sauce, sugar, rice vinegar, and chili flakes (if using). Stir and cook for another 2-3 minutes to create a garlic sauce.
3. Grill or pan-fry the hot dog sausages until heated through.
4. Toast the hot dog buns lightly and place a sausage in each bun.
5. Spoon the garlic sauce over the sausages and garnish with chopped cilantro and pickled mustard greens if desired.

6. Serve immediately.

Pork and Chinese Cabbage Stew

Ingredients:

- 1 lb pork shoulder or belly, cut into cubes
- 1/2 head Chinese cabbage, chopped
- 2 carrots, sliced
- 4 cloves garlic, minced
- 1 thumb-sized piece ginger, sliced
- 4 cups chicken broth
- 2 tbsp soy sauce
- 1 tbsp rice wine
- 1 tbsp sugar
- 1 tbsp sesame oil
- Salt and pepper to taste

Instructions:

1. Heat sesame oil in a large pot over medium-high heat. Add the pork cubes and brown on all sides.
2. Add garlic, ginger, carrots, and Chinese cabbage to the pot. Stir-fry for 2-3 minutes.
3. Pour in the chicken broth, soy sauce, rice wine, and sugar. Bring to a boil, then reduce heat and simmer for 1-1.5 hours until the pork is tender.
4. Season with salt and pepper to taste.

5. Serve hot, garnished with chopped green onions if desired.

Sweet Soy Braised Chicken

Ingredients:

- 4 bone-in, skin-on chicken thighs
- 1/4 cup soy sauce
- 1/4 cup rice wine
- 2 tbsp sugar
- 1 tbsp sesame oil
- 3 cloves garlic, minced
- 2 star anise
- 1/2 tsp five-spice powder
- 1/4 cup green onions, chopped
- 2 tbsp cornstarch (optional, for thickening)

Instructions:

1. Heat sesame oil in a large pan over medium-high heat. Add chicken thighs and cook until browned on both sides.

2. Add garlic, soy sauce, rice wine, sugar, star anise, and five-spice powder to the pan. Stir to combine.

3. Lower the heat, cover, and let the chicken braise for 30-40 minutes, turning occasionally until tender.

4. Optional: Mix cornstarch with a little water to create a slurry, and add it to the pan to thicken the sauce.

5. Remove the chicken and reduce the sauce if necessary. Pour the sauce over the chicken, and garnish with chopped green onions.

6. Serve with steamed rice.

Roasted Eggplant with Soy Sauce

Ingredients:

- 2 medium eggplants, sliced into rounds or lengthwise
- 2 tbsp soy sauce
- 1 tbsp sesame oil
- 1 tbsp honey or sugar
- 2 cloves garlic, minced
- 1 tbsp rice vinegar
- 1/2 tsp chili flakes (optional)
- 1 tbsp sesame seeds (optional)
- Chopped green onions for garnish

Instructions:

1. Preheat your oven to 400°F (200°C).
2. Arrange the eggplant slices on a baking sheet. Drizzle with sesame oil and season with salt.
3. Roast for 20-25 minutes, flipping halfway through, until the eggplant is tender and slightly golden.
4. While the eggplant is roasting, mix soy sauce, honey, garlic, rice vinegar, and chili flakes in a small bowl.
5. Once the eggplant is roasted, drizzle the soy sauce mixture over the eggplant.
6. Garnish with sesame seeds and chopped green onions before serving.

Taiwanese Fried Stinky Tofu

Ingredients:

- 1 block of stinky tofu (available at Asian markets)
- 2 tbsp soy sauce
- 2 tbsp rice vinegar
- 1 tsp sugar
- 1/4 tsp ground white pepper
- 1 cup cornstarch
- Vegetable oil for frying
- Pickled cabbage for serving (optional)

Instructions:

1. Drain the stinky tofu and cut it into small squares or rectangles.
2. In a small bowl, combine soy sauce, rice vinegar, sugar, and white pepper to make the dipping sauce.
3. Coat the tofu pieces in cornstarch, shaking off the excess.
4. Heat oil in a deep pan or wok over medium-high heat. Fry the tofu pieces until golden brown and crispy, about 3-4 minutes.
5. Remove the tofu from the oil and drain on paper towels.
6. Serve the fried tofu with the dipping sauce and pickled cabbage.

Glutinous Rice Balls with Black Sesame

Ingredients:

- 1 cup glutinous rice flour
- 1/2 cup water
- 1/4 cup black sesame paste
- 2 tbsp sugar
- Cornstarch for dusting

Instructions:

1. In a bowl, combine glutinous rice flour and water. Mix until a dough forms.
2. Divide the dough into small portions and roll them into balls.
3. Make a small indentation in each ball and fill with black sesame paste and sugar. Seal the dough around the filling.
4. Bring a pot of water to a boil. Gently drop the rice balls into the water and cook for 5-7 minutes or until they float to the surface.
5. Remove the rice balls with a slotted spoon and dust with cornstarch to prevent sticking.
6. Serve warm.

Fried Taro Balls

Ingredients:

- 1 lb taro root, peeled and diced
- 1/2 cup glutinous rice flour
- 1/4 cup sugar
- 1/4 tsp salt
- 1 tbsp cornstarch
- Vegetable oil for frying

Instructions:

1. Steam the taro root until tender, about 15-20 minutes. Mash the taro root until smooth.
2. In a bowl, combine the mashed taro, glutinous rice flour, sugar, salt, and cornstarch. Mix until a dough forms.
3. Roll the dough into small balls, about 1 inch in diameter.
4. Heat vegetable oil in a frying pan over medium heat. Fry the taro balls until golden brown, about 3-4 minutes.
5. Remove the taro balls from the oil and drain on paper towels.
6. Serve warm.

Ginger Pork Soup

Ingredients:

- 1 lb pork shoulder, sliced thinly
- 2 tbsp soy sauce
- 1 tbsp rice wine
- 1 tbsp sesame oil
- 2-3 slices ginger
- 4 cups chicken broth
- 2 green onions, chopped
- Salt to taste

Instructions:

1. Heat sesame oil in a pot over medium heat. Add the sliced pork and cook until browned.
2. Add the ginger slices, soy sauce, and rice wine to the pot, and stir to combine.
3. Pour in the chicken broth and bring to a boil.
4. Reduce the heat and simmer for 30-40 minutes until the pork is tender.
5. Season with salt to taste and garnish with chopped green onions.
6. Serve hot.

Red Yeast Rice Pork Belly

Ingredients:

- 1 lb pork belly, cut into cubes
- 2 tbsp red yeast rice powder (available at Asian markets)
- 2 tbsp soy sauce
- 1 tbsp rice wine
- 1 tbsp sugar
- 1 star anise
- 2 cloves garlic, minced
- 1/2 cup water
- 1 tbsp sesame oil
- Chopped green onions for garnish

Instructions:

1. Heat sesame oil in a pan over medium-high heat. Add the pork belly cubes and cook until browned on all sides.
2. Add the garlic, red yeast rice powder, soy sauce, rice wine, sugar, and star anise. Stir to coat the pork belly.
3. Pour in the water and bring to a simmer. Cover and let cook for 45 minutes to 1 hour until the pork is tender and the sauce has thickened.
4. Remove the star anise and discard.
5. Garnish with chopped green onions and serve.

www.ingramcontent.com/pod-product-compliance
Lightning Source LLC
LaVergne TN
LVHW081319060526
838201LV00055B/2356